What is a Key Word?

A *Key Word* is a ██████████████████████ n by sight. They are t██████████████████████ they appear so often. ██████████████████████ *Key Words* so whatev██████████████████████ se books will suppor██████████████████████ will be learning and deve██████████████████████ cy.

Although *Key Wo...* ...are so common they are not always easy to learn. Most children find it much harder to remember 'the' than 'apple'. One of the reasons for this is that mentally they can make a picture of an apple, but they cannot make a mental picture for 'the'. Your child will need lots of encouragement.

What is an Incidental Word?

Other words, which are not *Key Words*, are introduced in the stories. This has been done to develop the second of the reading skills, that is, 'context'. The idea is that your child should try to guess the word by a) looking at the picture, b) thinking of a word which would make sense in the context of the sentence and story, and c) looking at the first letter of the word and thinking of a word that makes sense and starts with the right sound. Your child does not need to remember incidental words.

Attempting to read unknown words is very important. It is essential that you give your child lots of praise for a sensible guess. Never criticise an attempt, however wild. If the guess is wrong, supply the correct word, while praising the attempt.

Create a Feeling of Success

Your child must feel a sense of achievement for everything he/she reads. No matter how simple you think it is, give masses of praise. Young children need to feel that things are easy for them. If your child finds reading difficult, proceed very gently; find something which is easy so that he/she can develop a sense of success. Then you can pile on the praise and he/she will want to do more. Above all, don't push at this early stage. Keep it light-hearted and fun.

How to Use This Book

1. Write down the *Key Words* and show them to your child. Discuss the shape of the word, how many letters, what letter each starts with, etc. Write the words on separate cards and see if your child can learn one or two before starting the book. Find a page where a particular word appears and ask your child to point to the word.

2. If your child is quite confident, he/she might be happy to read straightaway. Otherwise, read the story aloud to your child first, pointing to each word as you do so. Spend time talking about the pictures because a great deal of the story is told in the pictures.

3. Ask questions, such as, 'What do you think will happen next?' Or 'Why did she do that?'

4. When your child starts to read the book, be very patient and encouraging. Never let him/her struggle over a word. Tell him/her what the word is.

5. Once you have reached the end of the book, encourage your child to read it as often as possible. One reading is not enough to learn the *Key Words*.

6. Use any of the activities suggested on page 28.

7. The text is specially designed to be read by a child who only knows the *Key Words* taught in this reading series. For this reason, you should start with the books in Level One and progress in order.

8. Avoid pressure and stress at all costs. Reading is fun.

Key Words introduced in this book:

going looked old Everyone
some man him

Incidental Words:

**trip museum bike touch toys clothes football
surprised talk time bus broken**

5

I can learn

Key Words
readers
Sam at the museum

Written by Nicola Morgan MA
an experienced teacher with a diploma in literacy teaching
Illustrations by Sara Silcock

Give lots of praise for reading, and stick the gold star
reward sticker at the bottom of each right-hand page.

Key Words are printed in the coloured band at the
foot of the page for the parent's reference.

Series editor: Nina Filipek
Series designer: Paul Dronsfield
Copyright © 1999 Egmont World Limited.
All rights reserved.
Published in Great Britain in 1999 by
Egmont World Limited, Deanway Technology Centre,
Wilmslow Road, Handforth, Cheshire SK9 3FB.
Printed in Germany.
ISBN 0 7498 4103 6

Museum
open
now

The children were going on a
school trip.

They were going to a museum.

going

They looked at an old bike.

Penny
Farthing

Everyone wanted to touch the
old bike.

looked   old   Everyone

They looked at some old toys.

Toys

Everyone wanted to touch the old toys.

They looked at some
old clothes.

Everyone wanted to touch the
old clothes.

Oh no! The old man was real.

Sam saw an old football.

man

It was my football, said the
old man.